I0156668

Reviews

One of Marilyn O'Leary's insightful poems begins with the lines "In the tumbler of a long marriage we smoothed each other's sharp edges."

Those lines spoke to me so clearly about my own 35 year marriage. They made me reflect on our sharp edges and the process of a life together that sometimes feels like being worn down and sometimes feels like being smoothed. O'Leary's ability to capture the complexities of a long relationship and the grief when it ends is valuable for all of us. I enthusiastically recommend her book of poems titled *No One To Wake*.

—Carolina Yahne, Psychologist

A powerful and beautiful collection of 48 poems about love and loss, written after the death of the author's husband. Reading this restored my faith in the power of words.

—Aanya Adler Friess, Dancer, Poet

other works by
Marilyn C. O'Leary

marilynoleary.com

No One to Wake

No One to Wake

MARILYN C. O'LEARY

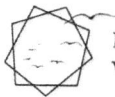

Mercury HeartLink
www.heartlink.com

No One to Wake

Introduction

When my husband of 50 years died after a long period of medical complications following a liver transplant, I was astounded by the emotions I felt that I did not want to talk about. To understand what I was experiencing, I wrote a poem almost every day for two months starting with the day after he died. Some days there were complete poems, some days only a few lines. This book includes many of these poems, in addition to others written in the following months. These pages recount the experience of reflecting on the life we had together, what it was like to be alone for the first time, and wondering who I would become without Jim.

March 9, 2013

On the day of our 50th wedding anniversary
I had to put sliced cucumbers on my eyes
to shrink the puffiness.

Your feet were hurting.
You felt you couldn't stand.
But we went to the party
planned by our children.
My eyes were better.
You could stand.

We were showered with blessings,
love and good wishes.

Then, seven months later, you left your body.
Now you're the light shining in the clouds,
the leaves rustling in the wind,
the river swirling in the eddy.

You're a paradox.
Here and not here.
You who believed and didn't.
You had faith in yourself —
in me, in our children.
You were rarely afraid.

March 10

How will I remember
that sweet, slightly yeasty smell
of your neck,
like cinnamon dough waiting to be baked.

I don't want to forget it —
it always smelled good
no matter when, no matter
what challenges your body was battling.

It was that soft little place
right beneath your ear.
You let me put my nose there
whenever I wanted.

A lifetime of having a special space
to nestle in when I was scared.

How will I remember that everything's OK
without you to tell me
or to believe
that you'll always be near
when you aren't.

MARCH 11

One thing follows another.
My poetry group met in the Jemez Mountains in January.
We all got sick.
When I went home you got your last illness
    —a week in the hospital
    —a month at home
    —two days dying.
Otherwise you lived every day
as fully as your body would let you,
using your bright mind.

MARCH 12

In the tumbler of a long marriage
we smoothed each other's sharp edges.
Most of the time we didn't know
what we were doing.

I scoured rivers, searching
for the perfect smooth rock.
I never found it.

Our windows look out to
granite mountains, soft-appearing
though they are hard and rough in places.
We have to keep them in our view,
a reminder of paths taken
cliff faces climbed or avoided
the timelessness of nature.

March 15

A week has passed.
I've spent it planning,
making arrangements.

How do I plan
or arrange
my life now?

There's room for the dog on the bed.
I can keep the window open.
The walker and hospital bed are gone.
I wish I could get rid of the shame and embarrassment
of my private thoughts as easily.

My brothers help me straighten and put things away.
We're like children rehearsing a play
but the props are flowers and an urn.

MARCH 16

No matter how many pictures we have
we can't capture you.
You were too many.
Even I didn't know all of you.
You hid yourself in your writings
and pretended to be an ordinary man.

MARCH 17

Pretty soon there will be no one
to wake up with a light turned on
in the middle of the night.
My brother and sister will be gone.

You are gone —
your ashes now in a box
heavy on the buffet
—flowers all around.

You took your leave
breathing like a fish,
swimming out into an ocean
of darkness and love.

We watched from the shore
and waved goodbye
as you disappeared into the sea.

MARCH 18

Too many papers and magazines to read.
It's all fallen to me.
How can I get to all of them?
Use the time I spent with you,
the time cooking for you,
being with you.
You used to tell me what I needed to read
and give me synopses of the rest.
You understood the Middle East, I never did.
I never could have got through the election news
without you.

I need to change my verbs to the past tense.

My to-do lists are different now.

March 19

No one to wake with my coughing.
No one to bother with the light.
No one to hear me cry.

March 20

Headache pain.
I can't get it to stop.

March 22

Sadness is an opening,
a soft place
a wrinkle in a sheet
avoided yet safe.
Once you put your nose in
the warmth calls you in farther
till you find yourself
unwrapped.

MARCH 23

Stiff neck.
Thinking of who's not here.
Dreams like a sitcom.

At our friends
      I miss you
At the table
      I miss you
Watching the news
      I miss you
Reading the paper
      I miss you.

I don't have the right dress
to wear to the memorial service —
not the right shoes, either.

Will someone tell me how to do this?

March 24

We memorialized your life —
the boy of 12,
 high school,
Notre Dame.
(I tucked our early years together into my pocket.)
You were a teacher, a father,
an adventurer, a risk-taker.
You got more real as you got older.
You loved your home and your community
and they loved you back.
You weren't sweet, but you were true,
living your own unique life,
freed to love
and be loved as you were.

March 25

Fatigue, memories, talking.

A bouquet of mourning.

Tears, emptiness, dreams.

The past is brought into relief.
The present is lonely.
The future is incomprehensible.

At some point it ceases being about you
and it is only about loss.
It is a deep canyon of loneliness.

March 26

The life we had together
begins to unravel like the cuff
of an old sweater. I see the thread
and look at it and know what it is.
I pull on it gently and it separates
from the sleeve.

But I still walk across the room to sleep on
my side of the bed.
Your books are on your nightstand.

I am alone without you now.
I am free,
but I don't know it yet.
I could do anything.
I could be anything.
I could go anywhere.
What if it wasn't you
who kept me tethered?

If I unravel the sweater what do I have?
Old yarn imprinted with the old pattern.
Being "not married" can be almost the same
as being "married."
If you make a new sweater out of the old

you will have too much of the old.
Fold the old sweater.
Wrap it in beautiful tissue.
Keep it as a remembrance.

March 27

The day we had planned to return from Hawaii
was the day you died.

You declared it a beautiful day.

The sun was shining
but that's not what made it beautiful to you.
It was because it was another day
given to you to live
and that day to finally say goodbye
to your precious world.

Our relationship was whole.
I saw the bad with the good
and reminded you of it.
You weren't a saint to me
but a man.
Of course I took you for granted.
Where did your love for me fit into your hierarchy?
We had a working relationship.
We worked at our marriage
yet for months would leave it alone
like a discarded blanket on the
corner of the bed.

You decided to leave on that beautiful day.
You made it easy, taking your last breath
at dinnertime, when we were all there
and could be with you.
You didn't disturb our sleep.

I see now that not only is every strength a weakness,
but every weakness is a strength.
You didn't have to be the best,
the loudest, the most noticed,
but you were the presence.
You were a man who listened
and so people fell in love with you.
No one in a room of conversation
would drown if you were there.
You always had a hand out,
a lifeline, a word.

The day you left you closed the circle.
It was a wonderful day to die.

MARCH 30

Last night
when I got up
in the middle of the night
I turned on the light.

MARCH 31

Time is the currency of love.
You asked me to sit with you
in the morning —
our morning routine, you said.
We were together with our coffee,
you in your bed,
I in a chair pulled up close.

Did I help you enough?
Did I love you enough?
Did I give you enough of my time?

I loved you as much as I could.
I loved you a lot.

April 1

"...and my coiled ear tuned..."
Stanley Kunitz, *The Testing Tree*

The morning is still dark.
I don't want you to visit, to scare me.
    I would never scare you.
What am I afraid of, ghosts?
You as a ghost? The ghost of what?
I want you with me still.
I feel your love, protection,
even your advice.

I've been told your passing was like
a supernova, exploding love.
I still feel it.
I felt your arms around me
as I tried to go back to sleep.
    I would never scare you.

I see you in the morning sun
feathering the clouds in pink,
in chamisa in our yard turning green.

I know you're all around,
keeping me safe
watching over me.

April 3

"The person you have lost is still here..."
Thich Nhat Hanh, *You Are Here*

I'm busy as if I have to get everything done
before you come back.
I made pancakes for myself yesterday,
muffins today. Your kind of breakfasts.
I placed a muffin in front of your photograph.
You are still here in memory, in spirit.
You are still protecting me.
Yesterday I was thinking about the doctor and hospital
visits,
the x-rays, MRIs, CAT scans,
the times you would start a project
then have to quit—
and would start again
and again.
I never realized how difficult it was
for you to come back.
Your will to live gave you the strength.
Thirty years of illness, crisis, recovery.
You walked down the Grand Escalante of your own life,
from plateau to plateau.
When you got to the river
you drank deeply from the water of relief.

April 4

> "...determined to save
> the only life you could save."
>   Mary Oliver, *The Journey*

You saved your life,
the life of a writer, a teacher,
an educator.

You led people out of themselves
to help them know
who they were.

They loved you,
they ignored you,
they disappointed you.

They extolled and eulogized you.

They came close and backed off,
like deer in a garden.

You never knew the extent
of their fascination,
for they were afraid and shy.

But you helped them
save their own lives.

APRIL 8

I am led to the gate of trust.
It is stiff from not being opened.

Inside the gate is love, comfort, help.
I am so grateful for being uplifted.

I am surrounded by a circle of love
from which I cannot escape.

I am piloting a magic ship.
I only set the direction —
the sea of grace supports me
and brings me to my destination.

I am blessed.

April 9

The clouds are wild and beautiful,
more promise of rain
than we've seen for weeks.
Is it enough?
    a pattern of drought
    a pattern of sadness
    a pattern of pain.
Where is the key that will change it?
What is it?

We sit with patience
and wait for rain.
Tears aren't shed either,
and headaches still come.
Is it all resistance to beauty —
to the cycle of life's beingness?

The wild and beautiful clouds
dissolve in the sun.

April 10

Look! I wanted to say to you yesterday.
Look at the mountains!
Clouds filtered in canyons
and behind crags to outline each feature
in ways previously undisclosed.

Clouds rolled over summits and down rock cliffs
revealing the beauty,
the majesty of the mountain.

When I stopped crying for you yesterday,
I saw you standing stalwart
near me.
It didn't feel like my imagination.
You told me you would always be with me,
you who claimed to be an unbeliever.
You believed in love.

The clouds have left the mountains
covered with snow.
It melts and seeps into the earth
greening up the trees.
I know where to find spring.
I know.

April 11

Your absence is a hollow space
that cannot be filled or soothed with tears.

It reveals exhaustion —
of meaning, of acts, trying, fear.

I hope behind the curtain there is hope.
Some balm to spread to soothe my aching heart.

People tell me I look tired.
This separation does not come like
tape ripped quickly from the skin —
a sharp, momentary pain.
No, rather it's skin pulling away from skin,
no easy way to do it
no place left unscathed.
Where it doesn't bleed, it burns.

But emptiness is worse.
It can't be filled with all the things
I find to do.
My morning coffee I used to share with you gets cold.
I begin my days alone.

April 12

Maybe it's not my heart death broke.
Maybe it's my foot — that's why
I drag through days feeling exhausted.

Something wakes me up at night.
I'm hungry but afraid to eat,
afraid my body will get heavier —
more to carry around.
I can't, with this broken foot.
I can't do it.

How long does it take a foot to heal?
A heart?

April 13

What can I do with this grief?
In the landscape of my life it's the climate.
But really, it's one stone on a necklace,
not the whole strand.
It's a diamond — hard, bright, important.
I can wear it or take it off.
It goes next to my wedding ring.

I still wear my wedding ring.
I've only been not-married
for .1% of my adult life.
And besides, what is "not-married"?
What part of life is that relevant for?
6:00 to 7:00 to watch the news;
Friday and Saturday, date nights;
Sunday dinner.
17 hours in the rain.

April 14

I am so well outfitted for
my journey of grief,
well-supplied with friends, family
good memories, love, comfort.

Having the right gear
makes all the difference.

APRIL 15

"...Touch me,
remind me who I am."
        Stanley Kunitz, *Touch Me*

At first these words pierce me, blame me.
Was it up to me?
Perhaps we can only be erotic in relationship.

I don't think so. It comes from within.
It is life. It finds an object, or the world.

April 16

The flowers, the plants
they echo to each other — still alive.
The clock ticks loudly.
I don't remember hearing it before.

Shall I clean out my closet or yours?
I'm the one called upon to change.
It doesn't matter to you.

I want to make a quilt out of your shirts.

April 17

Forty-three days since you passed.
An unremarkable number.
The peace lily from your brother
is finally opening,
a leaf of it burned as if by a child's
magnifying glass. Was it you?

I look for explanations.
The answer to all is Life.

I've already changed, been unafraid
to say my mind, and nothing bad happened
and I feel like a strong tree in winter
with all of its obscuring leaves gone.

It's all about me now.
I haven't cried at the mailbox again.
Today, tears seem far away.
I'm eating too much ice cream
trying to wrench my life from old patterns.

May 3

I lie in bed not thinking,
I think.
I don't think about you.
Then I think of all the things I have to do.
When I get up tears come.
Shall I let them be?
"It's a sad day," I think.
I have tears with my coffee
then think about getting a different coffee maker,
one that doesn't make so much.

My house is in disarray.
Most of your things are still here.
The office we shared is a mess,
your electronics, your notebooks half-filled.

Shall I put your ashes in an urn?
They're on my desk in a box.
I stack papers on it.

Today is like walking through heavy water.

May 7

Today calls to me
as I make toast out of what
some store names Sicilian bread (dried fruit and nuts).
It comforts somewhat, but I don't need much.

I am called to go forward,
to look ahead,
to not fear.
The impulse returns, beating softly in my veins.

I leave the grey silk shawl
draped on the leather chair.

It's time to plant the pots,
fill the hummingbird feeders.

When our lives shrank,
watching birds come to the feeder
became an activity.

Life today is about the
blue flax flowers that came up on their own.

I'd like to say where you are but I don't know
except that you stand by my bedroom door every night

with that smile on your face
and shield me from scary thoughts
so I can drop off to sleep.

What shall I do with your ashes?
I don't go to Baja.
The Rio Grande is too shallow with the drought.
Taos was never your place.
Maybe Pilar, by the Lorings' old house
or by decap bridge,
Coronado Monument, by the river,
the Place of Refuge on the Big Island.

The oceans are big enough
to take your ashes,
to transform them
to use them.
Maybe my last trip to Hawaii
will be to take these remains.

MAY 17
THE LITANY

From hepatitis C
> Lord, deliver us.

From shingles
> Lord, deliver us.

From Hodgkins lymphoma
> Lord, deliver us.

From a broken hip
> Lord, deliver us.

From gout
> Lord, deliver us.

From pulmonary fibrosis
> Lord, deliver us.

From atrial fibrillation
> Lord, deliver us.

From peripheral neuropathy
> Lord, deliver us.

From polyps, moles, warts, skin cancers
> Lord, deliver us.

From CAT scans, MRIs, blood draws, colonoscopies
> Lord, deliver us.

May 18

That drunken songbird is back.
It doesn't know where to sing or why.
It has no boundaries
no sense of decorum.
It sings early in the day and late at night.
It sings in the Russian Olive by the mailbox.
It sings in my back patio.

In my patio I notice
the clay angel holding a bird
casting a shadow on the
chair-shaped rock
on which a small metal Buddha sits
next to the cactus.

The cactus is ready to bloom.
Its spines annoy me, but
I wait for the payoff —
yellow waxy flowers,
the only bright color in
this desert green and red brick space.
I want to dig up the cactus
and throw it away
but it's an important part of the garden —
spines, flowers, then fruit.

My father brought prickly pears home.
I ate them. Now only coyotes
eat these.
I will see the big seeds in their scat
when I walk to the river.

It's a drought river again this year,
low, shallow, narrow,
barely moving.

I want to sprinkle ashes in the river,
but there's not enough water to take them away.

I don't know what to do with your ashes.
I haven't looked at them yet.
I move the heavy box from place to place.
It's now in the guest room.

Were you a guest there
when you died
breathing like a fish out of water
or like a woman giving birth
who practiced to make it easier?

You didn't want to turn our bedroom
into a sick room.
Your little considerations
sprinkled powder on my chafing skin
but I still have scars.

May 27

In this mixed bouquet of grief
        some bright flowers.
I bought you lavender roses today.
Some days are sunflowers
some are green leaves to fill in spaces
occasionally a starburst lily
some days a bud that doesn't open.

My life goes on. How?
My joke — after a funeral what people say —
"He was a good old guy. Where should we go to eat?"

But still the bouquet is there.

Our life together was a mixed bouquet.
Sometimes the flowers lasted for a while.
Sometimes they died right away.

Did we really do the best we could?
You? — me?
Sometimes it seemed to fall so short.
Sometimes it was like a dance.

May 30

> "The writer was the hero who went deep into
> the imagination and returned....If the story got
> published the writer could say to his readers, there,
> that's proof of my journey."
>
> *The Old Man's Love Story*, Rudolfo Anaya.

What does it mean
 to live my own life today?
When I look back I see so many clichés.

Yet I must sit here
and find words.

I am exhorted to live my own unique life.
It doesn't mean to take, to acquire.
But what does an old woman have to give?
I used to know.

Maybe it's only persistence —
keeping on.
"Give us a smile."

When you finally died
you made short work of it.
"Today's the day." Let's get it over with.

Breathe. Breathe. Breathe. Breathe.
As if you wanted to use up all your breath
as fast as you could.
No morphine. Don't slow this baby down.
Let's go.
Your last ride.

Can I live now without expectations?
What I expect you expect of me?
What I expect others expect?
What I expect?
Those expectations are like a magic box
with sliding sides.
Can I escape?

Words are the path, the way out,
but I don't know where they will lead.

JUNE 2

I don't want to cry today.
I don't want to be old.
I don't want to have a headache.
What's left?
Last night I put some books in boxes
but who can I give them to?
All the things we didn't talk about,
things we didn't ask for,
things we didn't do.
Last night I went out to buy ice cream
like an addict,
embarrassed, surreptitious.
I heard your voice.
"Buy the fucking ice cream."
I sat outside in cool night air
and ate ice cream that reminded me
of Hawaii.
You didn't like me saying
I wouldn't go back without you,
but it's too much a place for couples.
I'm uncoupled.
No one to go to a movie
on the spur of the moment.
Everything must be planned.
I'm embarrassed to call friends

—don't want them to know
I'm lonely.
I think about growing up
in my extended family
—now most are gone
and I have only one grandchild.
I think I should do without everyone
but they're like balm.
I need them.
Our son was here yesterday helping me —
putting in smoke alarms, window stoppers.
How to live alone.
What's gone won't return.
Grandparents, aunts
parents
you.
It always comes back to
not knowing what I had
when I had it.
Children shouting
men laughing
women talking
silverware clinking on dishes
warm smells of familiar food
too many desserts.
How can I give that up?
What do I have?
Today.

This minute.
The air brushing my skin.
The sound of a felt tip on paper.
Creamy coffee in a blue mug.
The ability still to appreciate.

June 4

Did I make your favorite foods often enough?
How little it would have taken
but my life kept poking through
like a tenacious weed that
pushes its way through a rock.
When did what I wanted matter?
That fear of losing myself in you
was terror, the horror movie plot of my life.
That urge, that necessity,
pushed out, came out
unexpectedly,
softly,
desperately.
The recipe for my life
had ingredients you didn't like.

JUNE 6

Outside, an angel with a bird,
a Buddha,
an Indian pot on its side,
space for an urn —
a tall golden vase
with birds and words etched on the sides,
your ashes
that will wait for mine.

June 7
(After Collecting Your Notebooks)

Your words,
voluminous.
Your love spilled out
your pain
your doubt.
Yet you were alight
with an inner glow
that knew no matter what
you were made for something
and some import,
that your life had meaning
even if it was only to please me,
to protect, to shelter, to love,
and still you do it.
How can I say I'm not worth it?

Divinity looks through your eyes
through my eyes.
To deny it diminishes all —
our divinity
—the personalness of spirit,
your words.

June 11

The emptiness of your leaving
does not bring me space.
It's more like the rain
that doesn't come.
I have stopped expecting it.
I have been trained by drought.
The weather now is wind, dirt, and fire.
Dust swirls into great and terrible clouds
and impairs my vision.
Fire does nature's work.

We don't get to choose our losses.
The desert creeps closer.
Do we adapt
or flee to find water?

June 12

My heart broke open years ago.
It made a space for grief.
Now grief has come again.

I want to be an alchemist for grief,
but it's not changing.
It just comes into my life
like a tall man
with an indistinguishable face.
It stands there
taking up space.

I have to make a place for it,
get used to it
because it is here to stay.
Trying to make it leave
could become a rude obsession.
Let it stay.
It will anyway.

June 14

The clutch of grief
comes in the morning
before I am awake.
Eyes don't want to open.
Throat is still closed.
Breath is weak.
Organs feel leaden.
Why doesn't the circle of old women tell you?
Because it's like childbirth.
The birthing of
an individual self
softens the pain.
Widows can clean their homes,
tend their gardens,
cook, maybe even knit, sew —
make poetry, paint —
make a life while waiting
for the heart to mend.

At the end is a door
that leads to another world.

June 25

You treated me like a queen
You were my knave
bowing before me
afraid of my anger
hungry for my love.

I was haughty, disdainful
rarely appreciating your faithfulness,
that you dedicated your life to me.

I provided you a hospice
a shelter.
You gave me loyalty.
You were true.
We could count on each other.

October 5

The door to the cage is open.
For days the bird only looks at it.
One day it hops out.
Now it stands looking at the cage.

October 7

Balloons again, the hot air kind.
It must be October.
I have a headache
and the damn balloons are up again
and you're dead and I haven't ridden
in a balloon
since my 50th birthday, when we went up
with that friend of yours, the doctor
who left his wife and her lovely crystal stemware
to live with the woman who had his little baby.
Well, we went up and came down.
I don't remember much of a ride
but at least we didn't get caught
on hot electrical wires, dumped out
on the ground unceremoniously,
and at least you didn't leave me
or I you, and there was no surprise baby
in the picture. We made it
through 50 years. I held on for dear life
and finally learned to enjoy the ride,
and you, who never seemed afraid,
left, using your breath to lift off.
I waved and waved till you floated out of sight.

Epilogue

Yesterday I wore your quilted vest,
the black one, Patagonia, I think.
I found a pocketknife, a pen, and a cough drop
in the pockets.

When I saw your birthday on my calendar
I was startled — how could there still be your birthday?
I'm ordering flowers for me.
The card will say,
"To thank you for all the wonderful birthdays you gave me."

Clouds hang heavy over the mountains.
Lights blink through the glass.
Are they reflected or are they really in the hills,
someone's home?

I claim you are with me
in a reality I don't understand.
You seem more than a memory.

Some friends condescend, believe I am simple-minded,
but how can that force that lived in you be gone?
It held you, you didn't hold it.
I saw that.

Look, the clouds are turning pink—
the sun still moving south.
All around there's color — a birthday gift
from you to me. I give you
my good memory.

You would be 74.
I would make you a chocolate cake
with white frosting and some
plain spaghetti with butter and cheese.

You would be simply satisfied.
Anything was enough for you.
The elaborate parties I planned
were just for me.

AUTHOR BIO

Marilyn C. O'Leary has worked as a water lawyer, teacher, and professional coach. She has authored two chap books of her poems and co-authored two anthologies, *Quartet* and *Quintet*, with her poetry group. She is also the co-author of *In Sickness and In Health* and *Keep Choosing.* She lives in Albuquerque, NM.

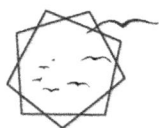

www.ingramcontent.com/pod-product-compliance
Lightning Source LLC
Chambersburg PA
CBHW031141090426
42738CB00008B/1176